THE NATIONAL PARK SERVICE
A Seventy-Fifth Anniversary Album

Monument Valley, September 13, 1935. Zeke Johnson, first custodian of Natural Bridges National Monument, is seated at right. Photographer unknown

THE NATIONAL PARK SERVICE

A Seventy-Fifth Anniversary Album

William Sontag and Linda Griffin, Photo Editors

Essay by Paul Schullery

ROBERTS RINEHART PUBLISHERS

*A portion of the sales proceeds from this book will be
allocated to two funds administered by the National Park
Foundation: The Horace Albright Employee Development
Fund, and The Fund for National Park Interpretation and
Education Programs*

*All photographs are courtesy of the National Park Service
unless otherwise indicated*

NATIONAL PARK SERVICE
1916 - 1991
TM

CONTENTS

Preface by William Sontag   vii

"The Service of the Parks": an essay by Paul Schullery   1

The Photographs

I.   THE RESOURCE   23

II.   PIONEERS AND LEADERS   41

III.   RANGERS AT WORK   63

IV.   TOURISTS AT PLAY   91

Acknowledgments   120

Newton Drury and Horace Albright celebrate the 25th Anniversary of the National Park Service on August 29, 1941 at Rock Creek Park in Washington, D.C. Photographer unknown

PREFACE

"The hottest places in hell are reserved for those who in time of great moral crises maintain their neutrality."

—*Dante Alighieri*

PRESERVATION VERSUS use. People versus protection. Habitat for bears or parking spaces for fishermen? Signs that admonish "Keep off the grass" and exhibit labels that invite "Please touch!" Access here, barriers there. Visitors to national parks are doubtless struck with what appear to be inconsistencies in the management of the resources they have come to enjoy.

For the record, park managers and National Park Service employees everywhere live with these apparent contradictions on a daily basis. Parks have never been static places under lock and key. Nature is intrinsically dynamic. Historic properties change despite all efforts to slow their deterioration. Visitor needs and demands swing like a pendulum, from place to place and from year to year. Changes and choices are the only constants in park operations.

And parks are only protected, visitors are only served when change and choice are partners. Indecision and neutrality are anathema to the continued protection and understanding of natural and cultural heritage.

Nineteen ninety-one, the year of the first edition of this book, is the 75th Anniversary of the National Park Service—the Diamond Anniversary of the "crown jewels." The national park system (begun in 1872 with the establishment of the first national park, Yellowstone) and the National Park Service (launched in 1916 by Stephen Mather and Horace Albright) may be properly thought of as siblings despite their difference in age of forty-four years. Their parents are citizens who recognize the simultaneous wealth and fragility of significant resources and legislators who acknowledge the need for a structure, a framework to manage and protect those resources.

Of the two siblings, "system" and "Service," the latter is the decision-maker. If it is true, as some have said, that "the mountains don't care," and if the appreciative citizenry is nevertheless untrained and poorly organized, then it falls to the Service to exercise care and judgement. It is only a matter of historic record that the institutional judgement of the Service has been uneven, sometimes pocked with errors, and inspired, timely and astute at other times. It is also fair to say, however, that the care provided by Service employees has been uninterrupted, despite significant fluctuations in the parental behavior of citizens and legislators.

Paul Schullery's essay, "The Service of the Parks" explores the historic and contemporary sociology of parks, gently and articulately. He describes the interplay and the intercourse between and among visitors, decision-makers and resources. Intimately familiar and having a little fun with his subjects, Mr. Schullery introduces us to these pivotal relationships—relationships which neither tolerate "neutrality" nor foster apathy. We see in his written illustrations the truth of Alfred North Whitehead's observation: "It is a false dichotomy to think of nature *and* man. Mankind is that factor *in* nature which exhibits in its most intense form the plasticity of nature."

In the accompanying photographic record it is equally evident that humans are nourished by direct contact—at work and at play—with their natural and cultural heritage. It is the hope of this book's publisher, author and photo editors that the text and images will foster a clearer understanding of what parks are all about, have always been about. National parks are outstanding wild, cultural and recreational places in which people may learn about, be inspired by, and contribute to the nation's resource legacy.

The parks will continue to serve those functions if—and only if—people continue to religiously think and express opinions about what parks are and ought to be. The very strength of the now seventy-five year-old National Park Service is the continued grappling with and vigorous discussion of its apparently dichotomous mission, "preservation versus use."

Bill Sontag
Lakewood, Colorado
March, 1991

THE SERVICE OF THE PARKS

Paul Schullery

The People Before

TSANKAWI MESA is part of Bandelier National Monument, near Los Alamos, New Mexico. From the mesa top you can look across a narrow valley onto the next mesa, which is known locally as "lab land" because it is in another federal reservation, the Los Alamos Laboratory. Scattered here and there among the juniper and pinyon pine on this neighboring mesa are stark, bright buildings and towers where all manner of secret and sophisticated research, especially in weapons systems, goes on. That sight alone gives pause, and in it people of every political persuasion will find something to think hard about.

But this is not a simple view. Let your vision drop from the forested and fenced mesa top, and slip over the abrupt cliff edges. Only a couple hundred feet down, where the sheer orange rhyolite cliff face meets the slanting lower slopes, you will see other signs of life. The cliff bottom is lined with ancient caves, where a thousand years ago the Anasazi who once settled this entire region carved homes in the soft rock.

There on Tsankawi, as you stand amidst still more Anasazi ruins, you are exposed to a hint of the cultural breadth of the American landscape. There on Tsankawi, it seems that for all the things that the national parks can illuminate for us–all the grand and subtle wonders of ecology, archeology, and history–for all of that, what the parks illuminate best is us. Those of us who come to these places with even the slightest mood of reception are quickly drawn into the setting, and look for some reflection of ourselves there.

In the tremendous wildland parks, visitors may, in the words of John Muir, "mix and enrich their own little ongoings with those of nature." The parks have always been treasured for the spiritual enrichment of their experience. But in the hundreds of smaller sites in the national park system, there are other kinds of enrichment, some more complicated, and many in which nature, or its appreciation, seems only a peripheral issue.

But at heart, it still is in some ways a nature-directed park system. If you go into one of the natural sites, be it Acadia or Lassen Volcanic, you are there to deal with the land, its life, and its processes. If you go to a prehistoric cultural site, be it Mound City or Chaco Culture, you are caught up in the response of some other society (don't for a minute fall into the trap of calling them "primitive") to the land. If you go to a historic site, be it Gettysburg or Fort Point, you are witnessing how we, in our own volatile civilization, came to terms with the land.

The national parks have been one of our age's greatest institutional experiments. We have succeeded in creating a system of reserves that accomplishes things beyond the dreams of national park pioneers a century ago. And yet if you read the dialogues that surround the parks, we seem to ourselves, in each generation since that daring beginning, not to be succeeding at all; the struggle to protect and properly manage these lands grows ever more complicated and contentious.

What we have learned is that the parks are an experiment that will never end; we will never get the data all gathered, and we will never close the laboratory door and write up a final report. We keep learning, we keep making mistakes, and we keep making what we think is progress. Perhaps most important, we keep at it. Like the people before us who struggled to come to terms with this land, we get no guarantees. And, like the people before, we are determined to do our best.

An Instrument of Social Service
ON A scrubby hillside near Mammoth Hot Springs in Yellowstone Park is the old post cemetery of Fort Yellowstone. Here, during the U.S. Cavalry's stay in the park (1886-1918), a variety of soldiers, their relatives, and other locals were interred. Many were removed for reburial elsewhere following the departure of the army, but a few dozen graves remain, shaded by grasses, shrubs, and trees that have recolonized the site over the years.

The headstones introduce a few army employees, a few hotel maids, a few miscellaneous names without additional information. Every time I visit there, I seek out one small marker that never fails to arouse in me feelings of mystery and loss; all the stone says is "unknown child."

Life was not easy in Yellowstone back then, and there's no accounting for this anonymous little life. One could build a hundred novels from it: a chambermaid's tragic romance with a soldier; a child separated from its parents and dead and forgotten for years in the wilderness; a saloonkeeper finds a basket on his porch on a morning after a freak snowstorm. Imagine the fictional opportunities.

Maybe it's because of that slightly maudlin and certainly melodramatic mood that this grave also sets me to finding large symbols in small events. Maybe it's because as a historian I'm too close to the obvious symbolic power of this grave. Whyever it happens, I find myself seeing the national parks here, too. If ever the federal government found itself custodian of an "unknown child," it was in the early days of the national parks.

If we proudly accept the notion that writer Wallace Stegner has proposed, that the national parks are the best idea we ever had, we had better at least admit that it was not an idea of any initial clarity. Yellowstone Park was created, without budget or sense of direction, in 1872, followed by the first California parks in 1890, and few others over the next twenty years.

By 1900 or so, it was becoming clear that these strange federal units, whereby the government intentionally withheld land from settlement and development while all around them land was treated in the opposite way, needed some orderly, centralized administration. A few, like Yellowstone, benefited from the protection of the military, in one of their least celebrated and most important civilian achievements, but no one, least of all the military, seemed to consider their custodianship a permanent arrangement.

Theodore Roosevelt, writing of the parks in 1912, said that, though we recognized the *city* park as "not merely an adornment, but an instrument of social service to the community," we still were puzzled by national parks: ". . .we are not yet sure as a people just what we want them for; and we have as yet given them no efficient and intelligent administration." He then quoted another great and now unsung conservationist, Horace McFarland, who complained that, "Nowhere in official Washington can an inquirer find an office of the National Parks, or a desk devoted solely to their management. By passing around through their departments, and consulting clerks who have taken on the extra work of doing what they can for the Nation's playgrounds, it is possible to come at a little information."

By them there was a movement to set up a "bureau" of parks, which Roosevelt suggested be called the National Park Service. This movement had its heroes, of which Roosevelt was decidedly one, though park history enthusiasts will have much more to say about McFarland, Robert Sterling Yard, Frederick Law Olmsted, Horace Albright, Stephen Mather, and others who did the actual legwork of getting the new agency off the ground following its creation in 1916.

"The service thus established," ran the Act creating the National Park Service, "shall promote and regulate the use of the Federal areas known as

Sixty-fourth Congress of the United States of America;

At the First Session,

Begun and held at the City of Washington on Monday, the sixth day of December, one thousand nine hundred and fifteen.

AN ACT

To establish a National Park Service, and for other purposes.

Be it enacted by the Senate and House of Representatives of the United States of America in Congress assembled, That there is hereby created in the Department of the Interior a service to be called the National Park Service, which shall be under the charge of a director, who shall be appointed by the Secretary and who shall receive a salary of $4,500 per annum. There shall also be appointed by the Secretary the following assistants and other employees at the salaries designated: One assistant director, at $2,500 per annum; one chief clerk, at $2,000 per annum; one draftsman, at $1,800 per annum; one messenger, at $600 per annum; and, in addition thereto, such other employees as the Secretary of the Interior shall deem necessary: *Provided,* That not more than $8,100 annually shall be expended for salaries of experts, assistants, and employees within the District of Columbia not herein specifically enumerated unless previously authorized by law. The service thus established shall promote and regulate the use of the Federal areas known as national parks, monuments, and reservations hereinafter specified by such means and measures as conform to the fundamental purpose of the said parks, monuments, and reservations, which purpose is to conserve the scenery and the natural and historic objects and the wild life therein and to provide for the enjoyment of the same in such manner and by such means as will leave them unimpaired for the enjoyment of future generations.

SEC. 2. That the director shall, under the direction of the Secretary of the Interior, have the supervision, management, and control of the several national parks and national monuments which are now under the jurisdiction of the Department of the Interior, and of the Hot Springs Reservation in the State of Arkansas, and of such other national parks and reservations of like character as may be hereafter created by Congress: *Provided,* That in the supervision, management, and control of national monuments contiguous to national forests

The National Park Service Organic Act, August 25, 1916

the Secretary of Agriculture may cooperate with said National Park Service to such extent as may be requested by the Secretary of the Interior.

SEC. 3. That the Secretary of the Interior shall make and publish such rules and regulations as he may deem necessary or proper for the use and management of the parks, monuments, and reservations under the jurisdiction of the National Park Service, and any violations of any of the rules and regulations authorized by this Act shall be punished as provided for in section fifty of the Act entitled " An Act to codify and amend the penal laws of the United States," approved March fourth, nineteen hundred and nine, as amended by section six of the Act of June twenty-fifth, nineteen hundred and ten (Thirty-sixth United States Statutes at Large, page eight hundred and fifty-seven). He may also, upon terms and conditions to be fixed by him, sell or dispose of timber in those cases where in his judgment the cutting of such timber is required in order to control the attacks of insects or diseases or otherwise conserve the scenery or the natural or historic objects in any such park, monument, or reservation. He may also provide in his discretion for the destruction of such animals and of such plant life as may be detrimental to the use of any of said parks, monuments, or reservations. He may also grant privileges, leases, and permits for the use of land for the accommodation of visitors in the various parks, monuments, or other reservations herein provided for, but for periods not exceeding twenty years; and no natural curiosities, wonders, or objects of interest shall be leased, rented, or granted to anyone on such terms as to interfere with free access to them by the public : *Provided, however,* That the Secretary of the Interior may, under such rules and regulations and on such terms as he may prescribe, grant the privilege to graze live stock within any national park, monument, or reservation herein referred to when in his judgment such use is not detrimental to the primary purpose for which such park, monument, or reservation was created, except that this provision shall not apply to the Yellowstone National Park.

SEC. 4. That nothing in this Act contained shall affect or modify the provisions of the Act approved February fifteenth, nineteen hundred and one, entitled " An Act relating to rights of way through certain parks, reservations, and other public lands."

Champ Clark,

Speaker of the House of Representatives.

Thos. R. Marshall

Vice President of the United States and
President of the Senate.

Appro'd 25 August, 1916

Woodrow Wilson,

national parks, monuments, and reservations hereinafter specified by such means and measures as conform to the fundamental purpose of the said parks, monuments, and reservations, which purpose is to conserve the scenery and the natural and historic objects and the wild life therein and to provide for the enjoyment of the same in such manner and by such means as will leave them unimpaired for the enjoyment of future generations." It has been, to put a new twist on an old phrase, a tough Act to follow.

Most of all it has been an Act that we never cease to tinker with. The original parks were grand landscapes set aside primarily to preserve geological wonders and spectacular scenery. In the succeeding century, these settings would acquire many new missions, of which I shall say more momentarily. But they also acquired some surprising sister sites.

Gradually the agency found itself in charge of other sorts of administrative units: national monuments, national historic sites, national battlefields, national historical parks, national cemeteries, and numerous other variations on the general theme that, however we may label them, we might as well call National Places of Such Extraordinary Significance for Some Reason or Other That We Simply Must Save Them. There are now more than 350 of them in the system, and the waiting list is not getting shorter.

In the process of all this growth the agency changed in many ways. In 1933, when President Roosevelt ordered dozens of military sites and monuments transferred from various departments into the National Park Service, he guaranteed that the National Park Service would never again be a simple, woodsy little outfit where all rangers could go to the same school. Now there are ranger-archeologists, ranger-sociologists, ranger-historians (my first title when I came to the agency in 1972), and many others. Few badges are expected to wear so well in so many trades.

As the National Park Service saw itself diversified, it also saw its overall, long-term mission come into focus. What started as a more or less unstructured attempt to save a few wonderful places took on a greater goal.

In the natural world, that goal involved saving representative samples of the various major landscape types that typified North America. Though there will never be agreement over just what all is representative, or exceptional, enough to fit into the goal, most national park enthusiasts would probably agree that we've come along way toward filling out the "wish list." There are still some important landscapes missing, but considering how late a start we got, we're not doing bad with this list.

In the cultural world, we have also made a great deal of progress, with hundreds of sites that represent, celebrate, and interpret many aspects of the human experience in the New World. Again, we are missing some pieces, and as long as we keep electing presidents, creating great art, fighting wars, and doing other historic things there will be need for new sites, but again we've come a long way. Considering that at the time Yellowstone was established virtually no one saw it as anything but a harmless, even trivial little government stunt with no real effect on the country, we have come an amazingly long way.

That is the big picture: the National Park Service exists to care for and even to help define our multiple heritages, from the wildest places that shape our view of nature to the most constrained urban settings that have been a part of our political evolution. The national parks exist to help us understand who we are, where we have been, and, once in a while, where we're going.

The Personal Park Service

THE AVERAGE park visitor—I've never met such a creature, but you know what I mean—does not often have cause to think about all this history. Any self-congratulation the National Park Service may indulge in about its significance is probably best kept to the administrative offices, because the visitors have more important things on their minds. The success or failure of this mythical average person's visit to the park is not going to depend upon history. It is going to depend upon people.

I have been traveling the parks as a major part of my life for some twenty years now, and I still have not lost that rush of anticipation many park-lovers feel any time they drive up to a park entrance station. For days before my arrival, I may have been traveling through glorious mountain or desert country, and there may be no perceptible difference in the country I see beyond the gate, but I still feel that quickening of awareness and interest. I have arrived at something, some place, really special.

If I have been there before, I find the warm familiarity of a place revisited—a bit of a homecoming. No matter how much time I spend in a park, its sights never grow old. In his hilarious book, *The Cocktail Hour in Jackson Hole* (1951), Donald Hough told of a conversation he'd had with an 80-year-old man who had homesteaded at the foot of Wyoming's spectacular Teton mountain range many years before. Hough asked him if he "ever got tired of looking at those same mountains," and the old man answered, "Those mountains are never the same."

But if it is my first visit, I find the simpler and perhaps stronger excitement of new country. That it has been explored a million times before does not matter; this is the first time it has been explored by me. Whether I know the park or not, I do know I am not uncommon in this: my senses become more attuned, and I work harder at soaking up the messages my surroundings are sending me. When we enter a park, we pay attention.

The first person we are liable to pay attention to is a ranger. In an age when most uniforms have lost much of the lustre off their old images, the ranger's is still remarkably intact, and the visitors still respond with interest and respect when approached by a park ranger. More than sixty years ago, Steve Mather, the National Park Service's first director, described these most visible representatives of his young agency:

> They are a fine, earnest, intelligent, and public-spirited body of men, the rangers. Though small in number, their influence is large. Many and long are the duties heaped upon their shoulders. If a trail is to be blazed, it is "send a ranger." If an animal is floundering in the snow, a ranger is sent to pull him out; if a bear is in the hotel, if a fire threatens a forest, if someone is to be saved, it is "send a ranger."

The spirit of this little appraisal has not changed, though the details certainly have–not all rangers are men now, and not all rangers jump to put out every fire that starts in a forest. As well, it is no secret that the ranger as an institution has undergone, and is still undergoing, evolutionary changes that are not always painless, just to keep up with the demands of a changing society. But the ranger still provides the public with a durable and often romantic personification of the best a life lived in and for the woods (or desert, or mountains) has to offer.

More important, the ranger is the personification of the National Park Service. Most people are only vaguely aware that the parks have administrators, or that the National Park Service has a Director, or that the parks employ numerous clerical people, researchers, and maintenance crews; but they all know that the parks are the homes of rangers.

Rangers are aware of all this. My favorite ranger story involves a legendary veteran ranger who was called on the radio by one of his subordinates; the younger ranger thought he needed advice on some sticky law enforcement situation he was embroiled in. The senior ranger's advice was simple, and complete: "Just remember who you are, and what you stand for."

So when you arrive at the gate, you have every right to expect you will be greeted by one of these singular figures, and usually you are. If he or she is doing good work, the greeting will be friendly, and the information will be accurate. If he or she is a really good ranger, the information will be given with pride. Rangering, at its best, brings out the right kind of pride, the sort that makes one humble. Few things can make one more proudly humble than responsibility. As the British essayist John Boynton Priestly wrote of one of his favorite American parks in the 1930s, "Every member of the Federal Government ought to remind himself, with triumphant pride, that he is on the staff of the Grand Canyon." That is exactly the mood visitors should encounter, and often do.

The late Edward Abbey, perhaps the national parks' most brilliant and admirable cynic, said that park visitors have three basic questions: "(1) Where's the john? (2) How long's it take to see this place? (3) Where's the Coke machine?" I, and many other past and present rangers, have succumbed to a similarly simplistic view of what America wants from its parks, though we all know better. If you visit a park, you really do need to know these things, or things like them. Sometimes you need to know them first. Sometimes you need to know them urgently. But once you know them, you file the knowledge away and get busy with more important things.

The national parks are ripe for sociological research, and some has been done, into just what visitors expect when they arrive, and to what extent they find it. Researchers have attempted to quantify why we go to the park, how we enjoy them, how we react to them. . . in short, what we get from the park experience. I find that sort of work interesting, and certainly helpful, but not especially complete. The park experience is of so many parts, and so subtle, and so personal, that questionnaires and interviews only capture flat little caricatures of the whole.

A friend and I settle into a park campground, let's say in the canyon country of the southwest. After the tent is up and the ice chest raided, and after the sun has lost its last influence on the sandstones and sages that block my view of all but the closest neighboring campsites, I sit and listen. There's a little breeze, carrying the tang of woodsmoke and the promise of a chilly night. Jays fly over low enough for me to hear their wingstrokes. Somewhere off to the west (assuming I still know west after winding through the campground's twisting lanes) I hear occasional bursts of group laughter; a park naturalist is holding forth with some success at the campground amphitheatre. Just up the lane, a family approaches, probably returning from the nearest of Edward Abbey's johns; the mother has obviously counseled the children on good flashlight manners ("Only on the ground–not in anybody's face, or at anybody's tent."), and there's some sense of adventure evident in their voices as they pass my way. Their feet crunch and shuffle the gravel with surprising loudness; every sound is magnified when there are so few sounds. Camping, so often associated with some simple communion with nature, is in fact a very social activity.

I take my fly rod along on a little hike up Bradley Fork, a small trout stream on the east side of Great Smoky Mountains National Park. Almost immediately, I enter a tunnel of forest; the afternoon sun filters in a hundred shades of early-spring green through the canopy, but nowhere does direct sunlight hit the water. In this soft, faintly glowing atmosphere, where backcasts must be threaded carefully between overhanging branches, I cast to deeper pools behind rocks, raising a tiny fish here and there and finally, triumphantly, landing a four-incher on a small dry fly. (It often happens that being successful in sport is largely a matter of exercising your sense of scale.) In this and other southern Appalachian streams, I am struck by the diversity of insect life; it seems that no two of the mayflies and caddisflies that emerge here and there from the water are alike. The forest around me is the same; a museum cabinet of specimens, dozens of types in a few acres, while I am used to the simpler plant and invertebrate regimes of the west. Though I made those casts more than fifteen years ago, I still often daydream my way up that little brook and marvel at its subtlety and diversity.

It is a typically hot, muggy south Pennsylvania summer day, and I am attending the grand finale of the celebration of the 125th anniversary of the battle of Gettysburg. I sit with an editor friend and his family in a crowd of several thousand listening to an assortment of speeches, songs, and presentations by sincere, history-minded people. Maybe it's the heat, but I can't get very excited about this, even though I'm a historian too. Then, at the end of the event, astronomer and peace activist Carl Sagan walks to the podium and speaks. I was initially puzzled at this choice of speaker, but now I understand. I couldn't quote you a single phrase of his message, but the spirit of it is still clear, that places like Gettysburg, made famous for a few brief days of hellish war, now provide us with singular opportunities to consider the meaning and beauty of peace.

I have scores—probably hundreds, were I to do an inventory through my disorderly mental files—of memories like these. Most park visitors do. Our park experiences are as complicated as any other experiences in our lives. The most sophisticated surveys cannot fully define them, and those of us who have them can only barely describe them. National Parks reach into every corner and level of our consciousness. They teach us, they test our imaginations, and they heal our spirits. They preserve things we love, and so we can't help taking them personally.

A Balancing Act

FOR SEVERAL days last spring, I arose quite early, a little after four, and herded a dozen or so equally early risers into a van for a short ride. They were my students, of all ages, at a Yellowstone Institute course in grizzly bear ecology and management, and we were out to see the bears. We routinely headed to one high ridge in north central Yellowstone, where we parked the van, unloaded tripods and spotting scopes, and stood by the road shivering and drinking coffee as we waited for the light to come. Then we spent two or three hours scanning the distant meadows and ridges, where, every day, we saw at least a couple of grizzly bears going about their daily duties. I'm sure most of us, even those of us who have seen a good many bears, are still thrilled by those memories.

One such morning we were joined by other park visitors in a minibus. After a couple hours of watching with us, these folks climbed back in their minibus and prepared to leave. As they did so, one of my students and I happened to have scopes trained on a sow grizzly bear with three cubs. She was lying on her back on a ridgetop at least a mile from us, nursing the cubs, as the little van's engine started and revved briefly. At the sound, she was on her feet, dumping the cubs unceremoniously around her, then leading them away into cover. A mile away, and she was still that spooky, and that easily affected by our activities.

Since we started creating national parks in 1872, they have been giving us an endless course in our environment. Especially, they have been telling us just how much, and in how many ways, we affect it: how the animals react to us, how the plants are affected by our management of the animals, how intricate are our involvements with the landscape.

At first, this wasn't seen as much of a problem. A century ago, we humans were pretty sure we knew what any landscape needed, and the parks were subjected to the same management most other landscapes received. We knew forest fires, wolves, and a variety of other natural forces were evil, and should be controlled. More important, we knew that human conveniences—roads, hotels, pretty photogenic meadows with peacefully grazing deer—were simply good, with no complications.

Over the years, though, without entirely abandoning our convictions about wolves or roads or any other aspect of a wild place, we have been compelled to admit that concepts of good and evil are deeply entangled with human value systems, and that these value systems can cause us a great deal of trouble in parks.

There have been many debates and dialogues over how to manage the parks, and a couple of primary questions have emerged; each debate may not explicitly focus on these questions, but they are in the background, all the time.

One is, How wild should the parks be? We have many choices open to us in deciding how to manage the parks, and many involve decisions over how much we can or should let nature manage itself. One extreme viewpoint has it that humans should intervene constantly, to maintain the landscape in some ideal state—a certain number of deer, or a certain number of acres of forest, or a certain number of fish in the rivers, or whatever—that best meets that viewpoint's definition of a good park.

The other extreme viewpoint has it that nature always knows best, and that we should always keep our hands off the setting; that it can be best enjoyed for its own ecological decisionmaking, and that humans by their mere presence can only diminish its significance and value by messing with it. I often tend more toward this viewpoint myself. I try to be calm about it, but that's very difficult these days.

There is a full array of opinions between the two extremes, and some people who hold one opinion with respect to some aspect of management may hold a different opinion with respect to another.

This spectrum of opinions is not new. For centuries, humans have struggled to come to terms with our dominance over the natural world, and our responsibilities to it. Western culture, for example, has worked hard to establish a comfortable feeling of superiority over the rest of creation, and at times has succeeded. As the historian of nature philosophy, Keith Thomas, recently wrote, "A reader who came fresh to the moral and theological writings of the sixteenth and seventeenth centuries could be forgiven for inferring that their main purpose was to define the special status of man and to justify his rule over other creatures."

But at other times, we have not been so sure, or so determined, about our superiority. The Industrial Revolution of the Nineteenth Century, freeing us from dependence upon the labor of "brute beasts," also gave us greater freedom to care about their welfare, and gave a long-existent humane movement an opportunity to flower. In the New World, the sudden possession by a relatively small European population of an entire continent (it needed only to be "acquired" from the even smaller population of natives) gave our little slice of western culture a remarkable opportunity, to start fresh with nature, and create our own system of relationships with it. From such powerful and diffuse historical forces came few institutions of greater challenge and promise than the national parks.

There is no telling how this will all come out. With luck, the dialogues that shape the parks will never end. They are part of our society's continuing redefinition of the best idea we ever had. But I can tell you something about how it's been going.

Gradually, and unevenly, we have been redefining the parks as places where human manipulations are kept to a minimum. In many ways, management for exclusion of undue human impact is simple enough; most people recognize the reasonableness of not allowing millions of visitors to collect rocks in a park that could too easily be damaged, visually at least, by such overuse. Few serious objections are raised to such obviously sensible regulations as those against rock collecting, the hauling off of prehistoric pottery fragments, or the cutting of live trees for firewood.

In other ways, exclusion of human impact and control runs up against our deepest beliefs about human importance and human values; some of the natural forces that shaped these landscapes are not easily accommodated in the modern world, and can cause us inconvenience or even harm. That sow grizzly bear with the cubs is no longer an object of admiration and curiosity when she is suddenly encountered ten yards, rather than a mile, away. In recent years, some people have even called for the removal of all grizzly bears from parks. Some wild things are a little too wild for some people.

But the overall trend has been for the National Park Service to find ways to manage parks so that human influences do not interrupt the fundamental workings of the landscape, and this brings us to the second question, which is How *do* people fit in these places?

Again, there has been a wide spectrum of opinion (it almost goes without saying that most of these opinions are, in the minds of their holders, backed up by scientific fact). On the one extreme are those who believe that humans, either native or European, have had so many effects on North American landscapes that there is no point in calling these places wild, or in pretending that we can ever separate humans from the setting. This viewpoint has it that humans are not to be excluded from nature, and are in fact a part of nature. This viewpoint has its immediate follow-up corollary, that starts, "Therefore, we should. . ." and continues to explain just how to manipulate the setting to the best advantage of those humans holding the viewpoint.

On the other extreme are those who believe that the parks and the natural processes in them can be respected, appreciated, and studied best when modern human influences are absent. This view has often been portrayed, and sometimes even with good reason, as almost anti-human; in its most virulent forms it implies that humans have, through an accident of evolution or simple bad manners, become something other than natural. It too, has a corollary of sorts, that starts, "Therefore, we should *not*. . ." and goes on to explain just how to manipulate humans to further minimize their effects.

Both viewpoints are at heart subjective, based on their adherents' religious, emotional, and cultural perspectives about what is best for the world. Both are also, in spirit, quite old, the subjects of centuries of human inquiry that have become ever more intensified under the scrutiny of modern environmental ethicists. And both are bound to result in frustration for their supporters, because the National Park Service is guided by a raft of legislative actions, starting with its organic act, that deny it the opportunity to go too far toward any extreme. It is safe to say that no extreme view is going to hold sway long when the agency's mandate so clearly directs it to serve all the people who hold more moderate views.

But, as I said a moment ago, those in favor of seeing the parks' natural settings function with a minimum of human influence have had their way in management more often than not. There is a very good reason for this direction, having mostly to do with our steadily increasing knowledge of the ecological character of the parks. Back before we knew that the best hotel sites and campsites were also often the best wildlife habitat, it was easy enough to usurp them for ourselves. Back before we knew anything about the complex roles predators and fire play in maintaining natural systems, it was easy enough to consider them harmful.

Now, with a wealth of ecological research findings to the contrary, and with a growing public enthusiasm for relatively whole natural landscapes, we have to think it over, and over, and over, adding new information all the time. If this doesn't cause us to face up to the real needs of the ecological setting, we at least must face up to increasing public desires for parks that protect their plant and animal communities in as whole a state as possible.

Though it isn't really fair or even realistic to expect the parks to be all things to all people, we can expect them to be quite a few things to most people. I agree with ecologist Douglas Houston, who in a landmark paper in *Science* in 1971 proposed that the parks can accommodate sizeable amounts of human activity without necessarily disrupting or destroying the landscape's character or functions:

> I contend that, despite man's intrusions into the ecology of national parks, the pristine ecosystem relations in many of them are comparatively intact or have some reasonable potential for being restored. This sounds incongruous, since visitors to several of these areas number in the millions annually. However, it is necessary to recognize that the uses man makes of these parks are largely nondisruptive and nonconsumptive; that is, man does not supply or divert significant amounts of materials and energy to or from the park ecosystem, and he is not a significant part of the food chain. There are exceptions in almost every park to the concept of nonconsumptive land use, but I think it can be shown that the objectives for natural areas are realistic and that national parks illustrate a type of land use that makes it appropriate to recognize a unique park ecosystem.

What makes this all the more challenging for managers is that each park ecosystem *is* unique, and each must have management tailored to its peculiar ecological personality.

The development of this kind of management is not simple, but it is important. The parks, whatever their earlier history or involvement with humans, are now recognized as sanctuaries for ecological processes. This is not an easy mission. Sometimes it may not even be possible; we still only dimly understand our own influences on landscapes, much less those of prehistoric peoples.

But it is a mission that focuses on the least subjective set of forces involved: those exercised by long-existent ecological processes that were in place prior to the arrival of Europeans. Those processes, too, were sometimes influenced by humans, who set fires, hunted animals, and otherwise affected the setting. Environmental philosophers and park managers must struggle with the questions of whether or not American Indians were a part of the "natural setting," and how we go about preserving that setting in their absence. For practical reasons, we may have to get along without those prehistoric human influences, but there is no reason to think that nature will collapse without them. The goal that has emerged over the past thirty years is to protect ecological processes, rather than to protect some arbitrarily defined primitive condition.

If we focus instead on human preferences or conveniences in defining the goal of the parks, we have a course of even less clarity. Who should then decide what is best for the setting? Whose idea for the parks' direction is most likely to "conserve" all those things we are aiming to conserve? There is no clear answer to these questions, at least there is none that is as ultimately satisfying as the answer that nature gives us. When we ignore what nature is trying to do, we are left with no single force driving decisions; every management action is up for grabs, and the ecological setting becomes the home of gardeners and zookeepers.

Naturally (if you'll pardon the expression), management will still be hard and painful, and subject to contention at every turn. We will always have to decide when we have, indeed, altered a natural setting beyond the setting's ability to reassert its powers and reactivate the processes that made it wild. We will have to continually apply the best science we can, to grasp the subtleties of settings we may not fully understand even after decades of close observation. We will be, as National Park Service biologist David Graber has put it, managing for uncertainty. We will be adding some risks to the national park idea, risks that the founders of the movement would have been mightily uncomfortable with. But we will also be adding greater opportunities for learning, and far greater chances that the natural settings we cared so much for that we set them aside will be inherited by our grandchildren in some shape worth being grateful for.

So the balancing act goes on. "Conserve the scenery and the natural and historic objects and the wildlife therein," the Act said, and "provide for the enjoyment of the same in such manner and by such means as will leave them unimpaired for the enjoyment of future generations." It said nothing about ecological processes, and it said nothing about millions of people visiting a single park in a short summer season. It said nothing about acid rain and other forces that can change a park's landscape from without, and it said nothing about the inevitable changes that a natural landscape undergoes over time whatever we may want it to do. Its framers foresaw none of these eventualities. Like most good visionaries, they dealt in main principles, and left the details up to us. We have a lot of work to do.

Beyond the Boundaries

THE MOST commanding structure in Shark Valley, in Everglades National Park, is a 65-foot high observation tower. From it, visitors can look out across a huge area of sawgrass and hummocks, the characteristic plant communities of much of this park. Some years ago, a couple of the park's rangers and I climbed onto the roof of the tower one evening, and spent a night alternately dozing and listening to the wild night sounds. Now and then we'd hang our heads over the edge and watch dark shapes of alligators ghost through the water of the canal that surrounds the tower, but our most memorable experiences were not visual. Even in the middle of the night, the Everglades is never completely silent, but it does get pretty calm, until suddenly there is a splashing nearby, followed by the squawk of some bird that did not watch its feet close enough, or the thrashing of some other anonymous victim of life's more dangerous moments. The high and slightly mysterious drama of these little episodes punctuated an ongoing chorus of birds that elsewhere in the United States would seem most exotic, but here are a part of everyday life. In my travels in wild places, I have heard nothing else as chillingly and yet intriguingly strange as the nighttime cry of the limpkin.

My friends introduced me also to the imminent peril of the Everglades. As threatening as it may seem to the new visitor, it is far more threatened by us. Wading bird populations are reduced to tiny fragments of what flooded the sky fifty years ago. Everywhere here, in an ecosystem driven and sustained by slowly moving water, there is less water than is needed. Human needs beyond the park boundaries compete successfully for water, and so the original richness of the south Florida wilderness is dramatically diminished. In the Everglades, as in many other parks, modern conservationists have raised the cry that "The park is not enough."

It has always been a matter of considerable importance to national park enthusiasts, and to the National Park Service, that the parks have a role to play in our lives when we are *not* on vacation. Originally, they were seen, rather as early city parks were seen, as societal safety valves, where people could go for a little R & R that would restore their spirits and allow them to return refreshed to the "real world." That role gave them a pleasant relevance to add to their other obvious mission of protecting interesting animals and beautiful scenery.

That role has by no means lessened. As Wallace Stegner recently wrote of the public lands generally, they are "a safety valve of the spirit, the most precious antidote to the spiritual demoralization that immersion in our industrial culture is likely to breed." Not everyone would agree with Mr. Stegner that our industrial culture must necessarily breed demoralization, but his point is still a good one. There is nothing frivolous or impractical about the national parks; they are as vital to our society as are our museums, our stadiums, and our churches.

But the extent of that vitality, like the ecological complexity that supports it, has been slow to reveal itself. Here in the last years of humanity's most boisterous century, we are still learning just what values the parks have. One of the great ironies of modern parks is that they, viewed so long as a refuge from the real world, are now being called upon to help restore and define that real world.

The national park movement that originated in the United States grew into a world revolution in nature appreciation. More than a hundred countries now have parks or similar preserves, and even this fabulous collection of natural and cultural treasures has been recognized for its inadequacies. It was inevitable that, once we recognized that the parks might serve us best if we left their ecological processes function unhindered, that we would learn more about those processes. What we have learned is that those processes do not respect our arbitrary boundaries. We have learned that most parks were not established with enough understanding of how entire ecosystems work, and that the landscapes in the parks are only part of greater landscapes that extend far beyond the boundaries of the parks themselves.

This knowledge has led, especially in the past twenty years, to a movement for ecosystem management. Many American parks are now seen as the hearts of greater wildland areas, and one of the greatest challenges facing modern park enthusiasts is finding ways to coordinate and integrate the management of entire ecosystems that may be under the administration of dozens of federal, state, or local government agencies, and may already be used for countless things, from farming to logging to recreation. The wisdom of Houston's statements about the ability of ecological processes to function without major disruption in the presence of modern humans is still applicable here, but the issues are infinitely more complex than they are in the simpler confines of a national park.

As we struggle to pioneer ecosystem management around our parks, similar efforts are underway elsewhere. UNESCO launched its ambitious Man and the Biosphere Program in 1972, to identify and establish "Biosphere Reserves" that will, rather like our national parks attempt to do, protect a "representative system of protected areas."

There is an impetus behind these programs that goes far beyond providing nice recreation or protecting beautiful places. It is an impetus of growing urgency, driven by rising international awareness of the fragility of the *global* ecosystem. National parks and similar preserves have added yet another responsibility to their list; they have become barometers of the health of the planet.

As most of the earth is subjected to more intense husbandry and habitation, the wild places, the remaining spots that are still relatively unchanged, are our only measure of how much we have changed the earth. In a thousand ways, the parks are providing us with what the scientists call "controls," that is, places that tell us what the earth was like prior to our great technological revolutions of the past few centuries.

An Alaskan park with great undisturbed glaciers or snowfields may have sitting in its ice the record of thousands of years of precipitation, and climate. Bird populations in the undeveloped habitat of a park may tell us much about declines of bird populations in similar but heavily populated country nearby. The worldwide decline in frogs, just in the news recently, may be illuminated in part by an examination of frog populations in undisturbed sites.

Disturbance is a slightly unpleasant word, but it is a word commonly used, and quite unemotionally applied, by ecologists. In the deep and tightly layered sediments of an undisturbed wilderness pond are ancient records of the land: pollen from many plants, that tells much about the relative abundance of various species in various past times, and thus about the climate that would support those species, and the animals that would thrive in that climate; charcoal layers that hint at former natural fire regimes; faunal remains that further flesh out the prehistoric biography of the pond's drainage basin.

There are many ways the parks can contribute to our understanding of the changes our environment is now experiencing. Evidence like this will be critically important to us in measuring just how much we are now affecting our climate and our future home on earth. Playing a role in diagnosing the health of the planet may ultimately be the most important mission the national parks ever have.

These are lofty thoughts, and heady ambitions, for government reservations originally established to do much more modest things. Many of us wonder if we have the collective wisdom to live up to our dreams for the parks. After all, it was as much by happenstance as by inspiration that we managed to create an institution that would prove so valuable, in so many ways the founders did not imagine.

As I have written elsewhere, the parks, so often characterized as great "outdoor laboratories" where science has accomplished so much, have also always been laboratories of ideas, where we have studied our relationship with our world. It is one of their greatest gifts to us (which is to say, one of our greatest gifts to ourselves) that they are sources of such abundant and diverse intellectual and spiritual stimulation.

Frozen Moments

THIS BOOK of photographs is a celebration of the people in the parks. It celebrates them through historical images spanning more than a century of park experience, and three quarters of a century of the National Park Service. Those average visitors I mentioned earlier are rarely thinking of the long view, or the global picture, when they drive in and set up camp or check into their cabin. The John Muirs, Theodore Roosevelts, Steve Mathers, Freeman Tildens, and a few others took time for the long view, but even the parks' great pioneers and defenders were quick to get out and catch a fish, or take a hike, or just sit on a ridge and let the last light of day fade around them.

Nor are most visitors liable to concern themselves greatly with this controversy or that headline, though to the parks' administrators and staffs—government and concessioner—it might seem their lives are spent in a steady turmoil of debate over how the parks should be managed. Truth is, opinion polls still rate the National Park Service among the most popular and trusted of federal agencies, and truth is, the popularity and trust are no accident. Most visitors aren't concerned about such things because they have no need to be; their experience is good, or better than good, and parks they visit live up to expectations.

I hope that you will be able to put yourself in these photographs. Look past the sometimes formal or posed photographic fashions of some past eras. Look into the faces of those people, and remember that the moment the shutter clicked they let out a breath, smiled at one another, and went back to doing what they were doing. A ranger posing with some visitors turned to them and said, "You know, that camera reminds me of a little experience we had with a bear here a couple years ago. . ." A driver looked at the gas gauge of his Model A and wondered if he should push on to Flagstaff before refilling. Young people in bathing suits turned from the camera and raced each other to the lake. That frozen moment may be all they left for us to remember their visit by, but it was hardly the most important part of the visit to them.

So look for life in the pictures; what kind of day was it? Was there a breeze ruffling the water, or the hair of the vacationers? What of the land around them? How would you feel standing there with them? Did the August heat bounce off the canyon wall? Was it suddenly chilly in the shade of a sugar maple? In short, try to unfreeze the moment, and put yourself into it. It may not be as good as going to the park, but it may help until you can.

It was 21 below zero when I drove east out of Glendive, Montana, and though I'm sure it warmed a little by the time I got to Medora, North Dakota, it was still the kind of hard winter day that Theodore Roosevelt would have enjoyed for the simple adventure of standing out in it. The ranger at the headquarters Visitor Center there, where most people enter Theodore Roosevelt National Park, went out back and unlocked the old cabin for me so I could get a look.

This is the cabin relocated from the site of Roosevelt's Maltese Cross Ranch, to the north. From these rooms he oversaw some of his ranching operations in the 1880s and 1890s, and wrote several books, including some of his best outdoor adventure stories. It was easy enough to picture him seated at the small table, perhaps scooting it a little closer to the fire as the wind pounded against the windows, writing letters and articles to be read by his family and friends far away.

Shivering for a frozen moment of my own in the shade of the unheated cabin, I wondered what he would have thought if someone had told him, back when Yellowstone stood alone as America's national park, what was going to become of that modest little experiment in government conservation. Or if they had told him that not only this rough little cabin and the land around it, but at least five other places that celebrate his life, would become part of a great system of parks. No doubt he would have been pleased, perhaps flattered into that quick laughter he was so famous for. But I suspect that what would have pleased him most would be knowing, not that he would eventually earn that sort of attention, and not that we managed to develop such a park system, but that it had come to mean so much to the rest of the world.

He was more than dimly aware of what it could mean, and had a better vision than most of how important these places were to us. During his presidency he summed it up about as well as anyone could have:

> Surely our people do not understand even yet the rich heritage that is theirs. There can be nothing in the world more beautiful than the Yosemite, the groves of giant sequoias and redwoods, the Canyon of the Colorado, the Canyon of the Yellowstone, the Three Tetons; and our people should see to it that they are preserved for their children and their children's children forever, with their majestic beauty all unmarred.

To that I would add that now, after seventy-five years of the most energetic efforts of the National Park Service and its friends, surely our people do understand the rich heritage that is theirs. They may not fully understand every piece of it, partly because it is still being revealed to us, but in the national parks they have built a source of understanding that, if we add only wisdom and love, will indeed serve us forever.

The first National Park Service Badge, 1908. Curiously, this badge appeared eight years before the Service was officially established.

I. THE RESOURCE

Because any discussion of the National Park Service must begin with the resource itself—whether it is a preserved western landscape or a commemorated battlefield of our Civil War experience—the photographs in this section serve as a reminder of the many things national parks represent to us. While it is not possible here to include all of the over three hundred units in the system, the images that follow do illustrate the geographic range of our parks, from Denali in Alaska to Castillo de San Marcos National Monument in Florida.

Old Faithful geyser, Yellowstone National Park, Wyoming, 1871. William Henry Jackson photo

Entrance gate, Denali National Park, Alaska, 1939. Photographer unknown

Bryce Canyon National Park, Utah. Date unknown. Photographer unknown

Visitors and cars along the road in front of the new Mariposa Grove Museum, Yosemite National Park, California, June 11, 1931. George A. Grant photo

Dr. Harold C. Bryant , perhaps the "father" of NPS interpretation, conducting a nature walk in Yosemite Valley, early 1920s. Photographer unknown

Chesapeake and Ohio Canal National Historical Park, Maryland, ca. 1960s. M. Woodbridge Williams photo

Above left: *Castillo de San Marcos National Monument, Florida. Date unknown. Photographer unknown*

Below left: *Swimming hole at Hot Springs National Park, Arkansas, 1938. Werner photo*

Glacier National Park, Montana, July 27, 1932. George A. Grant photo

Rocky Mountain National Park, Colorado. Date unknown. Photographer unknown

Left: *Sitka National Historical Park, Alaska, ca. 1960s. Josef Muench photo*

Right: *Standing Eagle, a Chippewa, shapes a peace pipe from Catlinite at Pipestone National Monument, Minnesota. Date unknown. Photographer unknown*

This 1896 photo shows the U.S. Geological Survey at work in what is now Badlands National Park, South Dakota. N.H. Darnton photo

Zeke Johnson, custodian of Natural Bridges National Monument, stands near a sandstone formation that was later destroyed by visitors. September 11, 1935. George A. Grant photo

Devils Tower National Monument, Wyoming, 1930s. George A. Grant photo

Grand Canyon National Park, Arizona, 1914. Herbert T. Cowling photo

Above: *Mount Rushmore National Memorial, South Dakota, under construction, ca. 1936. Photographer unknown*

Left: *The birth of a national park. These two images show visitors gathering for the dedication of Theodore Roosevelt National Memorial Park on June 4, 1949. George A. Grant photos*

II. PIONEERS AND LEADERS

John Muir, Stephen Mather, Horace Albright, Frederick Law Olmsted: these tend to be the names most commonly invoked when one speaks of the origins of the National Park Service. However, as the photos in this section will show, the growth of the Service (and of the park system itself) was also the product of the contributions of less visible personalities, from quiet private benefactors to native peoples who shared their land with new and altogether unique agents of the government.

Two early advocates of the national parks, Theodore Roosevelt and John Muir, view Yosemite in 1903. Underwood and Underwood photo

Founders, Both Philosophical and Practical

Franklin Knight Lane, Secretary of the Interior when the National Park Service was established on August 25, 1916. Photographer unknown

Right: Perhaps the two greatest influences in the development of our public lands policies are shown together in this rare photograph taken at Muir Woods National Monument. At left is John Muir, the philosophical conscience of the national parks; at right is Gifford Pinchot, whose utilitarian views on forest management guided the National Forest Service. Seated between them is Congressman William Kent, one of the drafters of the National Park Service Organic Act. Hauser photo

Left: John Muir in Yosemite, 1907. Francis Fultz photo

The early days of the National Park Service saw the emergence of a number of leaders whose influence carries to the present day. In the photo above, taken in 1926, the first director of the National Park Service, Stephen Mather, is surrounded by colleagues at Yosemite (J.V. Lloyd photo). Among the many assets Mather brought to the service was his personal wealth; in fact, he subsidized the salary of the Service's first publicity chief, Robert Sterling Yard, shown at bottom right at Yosemite in 1920. Perhaps Mather's greatest accomplishment, though, was the hiring of Horace Albright as his assistant. Albright, depicted on the facing page in 1919 as superintendent of Yellowstone (J.E. Haynes photo), later became director of the National Park Service himself and was a tireless booster of the parks throughout his long life.

Benefactors and Boosters

Augmenting activists in government were private citizens who played a key role in promoting—and creating—the national parks. Pictured at the top of the facing page is J. Horace McFarland, whose American Civic Association vigorously lobbied for the creation of the National Park Service (Kazanjian Studio, 1920s). Below McFarland is John D. Rockefeller, Jr. whose donations to such parks as Grand Teton, Great Smoky Mountains, Acadia and others were unequalled. UPI photo. Shown at the top of this page is Frederick Law Olmsted, Jr. in 1925, who with his famous father greatly influenced landscape planning in the parks.

A Gallery of "Firsts"

Above left: Capt. Charles Young, superintendent of Sequoia, in a 1903 photo. Photographer unknown

Above right: Yellowstone's first "game keeper," Harry Yount, in the 1880s. Photographer unknown

Right: Herma Albertson, Yellowstone's first permanent female ranger-naturalist, 1923. Photographer unknown

Facing page: Galen Clark, Yosemite's first guardian, 1858. Carleton Watkins photo

Early Personalities

Above left: Roger Wolcott Toll, Colorado mountaineer and author who served as superintendent at Rocky Mountain and Yellowstone National Parks during the 1920s. November 18, 1931. Photographer unknown

Above right: Ansel F. Hall, the first chief naturalist and chief forester of the National Park Service. He also developed the first educational division, photographic division, and established the first natural history association. Merrie Winkler Collection

Right: R.W. Rowley, the head guide at Oregon Caves National Monument from 1910 to 1951, stands at the caves entrance in 1936. Photographer unknown

Facing Page: The swaggering pose struck here by Frank "Boss" Pinkley typified the spirit of early NPS employees sent, often without financial or adminstrative support, to administer the vast public lands of the West. As "Superintendent of Southwestern Monuments" from 1923 to 1940, Pinkley's jurisdiction included eighteen national monuments. This photograph was taken on August 20, 1934 at Casa Grande National Monument in Arizona. George A. Grant photo

Pioneers in Interpretation

"Interpretation"—or, quite simply, the art of appreciating—co-evolved with the Park Service's more familar responsibilities as conservators and protectors. One early yet perhaps unwitting interpreter was William Henry Jackson, whose photographs of such places as Yellowstone and the Tetons confirmed early explorer's reports of the wonders of these regions. Jackson is shown at left in the photograph above at the 75th Anniversary of Gettysburg in 1938. Allan Rinehart photo

If the interpretive role of the parks had any true champion, however, it was most assuredly Freeman Tilden, shown on the right hand page. A consultant to four directors of the national parks, Tilden produced a number of books concerned with the preservation and interpretation of natural and historic places.

The Tradition of Research

The heritage of scientific research in the parks is perhaps no better exemplified than by the individuals portrayed on this page. In th photo above A. Starker Leopold (son of Aldo) stands between fellow scientists G.L. Collins and F.F. Darling at Umiat, Alask in the summer of 1952 (Lowell Sumner photo). In a pioneering study presented to the Secretary of the Interior in 1963, the "Leopold Report," as it came to be known, recommended that pe biotic communities be maintained in as near a primitive state as practical.

With their great names associated with numerous scientific papers research reports, and popular books, Olaus and Adolph Murie— shown here at left atop Cathedral Mountain in Alaska in the 1960s—stand as perhaps the two most prominent wildlife biologists to have worked in the national parks in the mid-twenti century.

Yosemite Valley, 1899. Julius Boysen photo

The People of the Parks

In the early days, park residents were not just the uniformed representatives of the government, but also those who came before—and those who stayed on as neighbors after their land had been purchased or otherwise transferred to the government as park land. The photos that conclude this chapter pay tribute to all the people who called the parks "home," whether Native Americans or custodians of the far outposts of the Service.

Navajo hogan in Canyon del Muerto, Canyon de Chelly National Monument, Arizona, 1934. George A. Grant photo

The Blackfoot Band, Glacier National Park, Montana, 1933. George A. Grant photo

Top: Mother and daughter, Yosemite, 1929. J. Dixon photo
Bottom: Custodian and Mrs. Bob Lacomb, Craters of the Moon National Monument, 1931. George A. Grant photo

Wupatki National Monument, Arizona. Mrs. Courtney Jones in her kitchen (ca. 1940).
Photographer unknown

Mrs. Janet Voorhees, boss of Low Divide Chalets, Olympic National Park, 1936. George A. Grant photo

Aunt Sophie Campbell, a neighbor of Great Smoky Mountains National Park, 1931. George A. Grant photo

Uncle Dan Meyers, Great Smoky Mountains National Park, 1937. Allan Rinehart photo

III. RANGERS AT WORK

Their sidearm could be a clipboard or a revolver; their work station could be as exhilirating as a fire lookout or as mundane as a steel desk in some nameless goverment building. They traveled to work by car, or dogsled, or horseback—or perhaps their work came to them. As the photos in this chapter illustrate, the history of the National Park Service is the story of the ever-changing roles of its people who, eschewing the numerical ladders of civil service classifications, were and are known to all the world simply as "rangers."

Ranger Leonard Heaton conducting a tour at Pipe Spring National Monument, Arizona, sometime during the 1930s. Photographer unknown

Before the National Park Service was established, the task of enforcing the law in the parks fell to the U.S. Army. In this photo of 1899 a fallen giant sequoia dwarfs Troop F, 6th Cavalry. Tibbets (?) photo

Enforcers and Protectors

The first rangers in Yosemite, 1915. George Fiske photo

Above: Fireguard John McGraw at Shadow Mountain Lookout, Rocky Mountain National Park, 1933. Photographer unknown Below: Breaking up a still, Great Smoky Mountains National Park, 1931. George A. Grant photo

A Ranger guides a bus through a snowdrift at Fall River Pass, Rocky Mountain National Park, June 14, 1926. Photographer unknown

Rangers releasing a young black bear after removing it from a picnic area in Yellowstone, 1958. Jack E. Boucher photo

Sculptors and Quarrymen

Among the unusual tasks of the National Park Service over the years has been the creation—or at least the enhancement—of a park or monument site by tinkering with it, a practice that seemed to ignore Theodore Roosevelt's famous admonition about building bridges over the Grand Canyon, that "you cannot improve on it. The ages have been at work on it, and man can only mar it."

Ironically, Roosevelt became one of the four U.S. Presidents memorialized at Mount Rushmore National Memorial, shown in the photo above as it neared completion in 1941 (Rise photos, Rapid City). Perhaps resignedly, Freeman Tilden likened Mt. Rushmore to the compulsion of man to make his presence felt on the face of the earth: "He may be expelled from the garden at any moment, but he will leave his initials carved on the fig tree."

However one views Mt. Rushmore, quarrying in the parks at significant archaeological or paleontological sites has always been an important function of the National Park Service. At the top of the facing page, Indians quarry at Pipestone National Monument in Minnesota in 1893; the photo beneath shows "preparators" on the quarry face of Dinosaur National Monument in 1955. Harry B. Robinson photo

Boy Scouts reconstruct remains of an Anasazi granary at Zion National Park, 1929. Stork photo

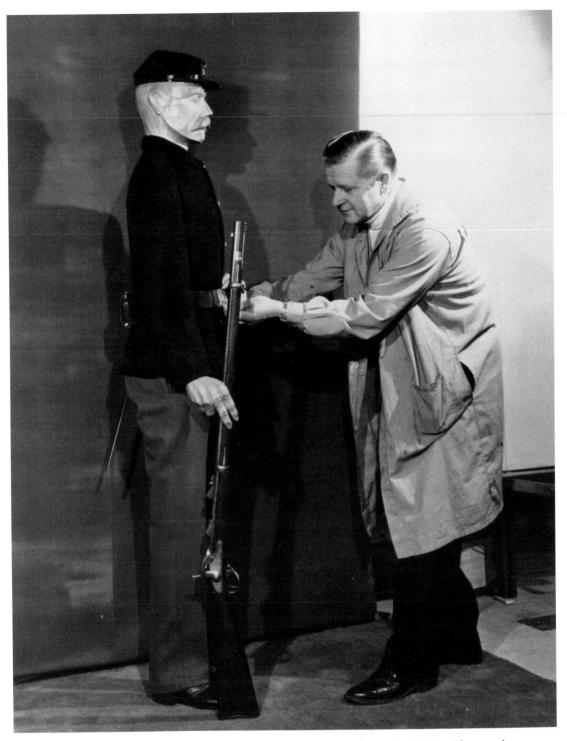

Museum Specialist Peder Kitti at work at Harper's Ferry, Virginia during the 1960s. Photographer unknown

The Mobile Ranger

Horace Albright and NPS Director Stephen Mather pose beside what is obviously the director's personal vehicle. Knowing the lean budgets of these early years of the park service, it is possible that Mather paid for the car himself.

Facing page: Ranger Wayne Replogle sits astride an elkified version of his government-issue motorcycle at Tower Junction in Yellowstone in 1932. Photographer unknown

Above: Yellowstone Ranger James McBride, 1921. Photographer unknown. Below: Rangers' motor equipment in front of dorm at Crater Lake National Park, 1941. George A. Grant photo

Building and maintaining roads was a never-ending job in the parks. Above: Turn-of-the-century paving operations at Chickamauga and Chattanooga National Military Park. Betts photo. Below: CCC crew constructing a turnout for cars in 1933 at Grand Teton National Park. George A. Grant photo

Shoveling drifts on Old Fall River Road, Rocky Mountain National Park, 1923. Photographer unknown

Above: Ranger Grant Pearson and sled team at Stoney Lake, McKinley (now Denali) National Park, Alaska, 1940s. Photographer unknown. Below: McKinley Superintendent Frank T. Been on winter patrol, 1940-41. Photographer unknown

Above: Toklat River Ranger Station, Denali National Park, in the 1920s. Fritz Nyberg photo

Below: Cabin and cache in winter, Denali

Outposts and Gathering Places

Facing Page: Ranger-Naturalist Landis before community building, Mt. Rainier National Park, 1929. Stork photo

Above: Museum at Many Glacier Campground, Glacier National Park, 1932. Right: Maltese Cross Cabin, Theodore Roosevelt National Park, 1963. Doudna photo

Facing Page, top: Temporary entrance station at Vicksburg National Military Park, 1934. George A. Grant photo. Below: Stephen Mather (left) explores a camp wagon in 1928 with members of a senatorial party at what was to become Theodore Roosevelt National Park. Roger W. Toll photo

Above: Nurse Phelps in front of the government hospital at Mesa Verde National park, Colorado, in 1929. George A. Grant photo

Left: Clingman's Dome Observation Tower, Great Smoky Mountains National Park. The date of this photograph is unknown, but the tower was torn down and replaced in the early 1960s. Photographer unknown

DEPARTMENT OF THE INTERIOR

NATIONAL PARKS

Sheet No. 1

PERSONNEL OF EMPLOYEES IN THE SEVERAL NATIONAL PARKS AND MONU-
MENTS UNDER CONTROL OF THE DEPARTMENT OF THE INTERIOR

Full name *Oliver P. Prien*

Born *Jan 14. 1876.* Place *Wisconsin*, *Dune.*
    (Date)   (State)   (County)

Education *High School two years at Wisconsin Univ.*

Legal residence *California*, *Santa Clara*
         (State)   (County)

Date of first appointment *July 15 1913*

Oliver P. Prien
       (Signature)

YEAR	TITLE	GIVE NATURE OF EMPLOYMENT EACH YEAR

1913 Ranger & Disbursing Agt. $1200.00 per Annum
Collecting Automobile fees to Nov 1st 1913.
Nov 1st -13. to Jan 1st 1914 Mounted patrol duty.

1914 Ranger & Disbursing Agt. $1200. per Annum.
Jan 1st to April 1st pruning and clearing of brush
in apple orchards.
April 1st to May 1st Mounted patrol duty valley floor.
May 1st to June Ant Post duty at Mono Grove.
June to Dec collecting automobile fees.
Sept 1st Appointed Chief Park Ranger.
Dec to Jan 1st 1915. On duty in office arranging
ranger dept. under new system.

(NOTE.—Use one side only; if more space is needed use second sheet; sign and date last sheet)

Biographical sketch of Yosemite's first Chief Ranger, Oliver P. Prien, 1916.

At the Service of the Parks

Above: Early Yosemite Rangers Charlie Adair and Billy Nelson have a howl over Park Service director Albright's book Oh Ranger! in this 1929 photo. Photographer unknown

Right: A summer working for the National Park Service has been part of the experience of many Americans, including this eagle scout and football player by the name of Gerald Ford. Thirty-eight years after this photograph was taken at Yellowstone, Ranger Ford succeeded Richard Nixon as President of the United States. Photographer unknown

Facing page: Karl Keller, an early ranger in Sequoia, in a 1910 photograph. L.F. Cook photo

An important naturalist at Yosemite during the 1920s and 1930s was George Melendez Wright. Wright was a crusader for habitat preservation and restoration before those concepts were in vogue. C.P. Russell photo

Another ranger-naturalist at Yosemite, Enid Michael, "dances" with a black bear in this photo taken sometime during the 1920s. Photographer unknown

Winter in Yosemite, 1926. C.P. Russell photo

Facing page, top: Washington, D.C. visitors at the "Nature Van," a "mobile interpretive unit" operated by Ranger Maurice Sullivan in the 1950s. Abbie Rowe photo Bottom: Interpreting history with children, Ft. McHenry National Monument, Maryland, 1950s. Photographer unknown

Mesa Verde Superintendent Jesse Nusbaum and friends, ca. 1925. Photographer unknown

IV. TOURISTS AT PLAY

This final chapter honors those who are served by the men and women of the National Park Service—the "park visitor," in the argot of the ranger. In addition to paying the bills for the Service for seventy-five years, park patrons should be recognized for happily tolerating changes in management philosophy that have taken us from the days of dancing bears to far less exploitive uses of the park resource.

View of the Grand Canyon looking West, 1930.
George A. Grant photo

Artist at Lookout Point, Yellowstone National Park, 1922. Photographer unknown

For the Benefit and Enjoyment of the People

Facing page: Horseback riders near Odessa Lake, Rocky Mountain National Park, 1916. Photographer unknown

Ice Cave on the Boulder Glacier, Glacier National Park, 1932. George A. Grant photo

From Ice-Bound Summits to River Waters

Tyndall Glacier, Rocky Mountain national Park, 1916. Photographer unknown

Ranger on trail with party, Bandelier National Monument, 1938. Allan Rinehart photo

Above: Visitors at Glacier, 1933. George A. Grant photo

Right: An early tour at Wind Cave National Park, South Dakota, 1903. Photographer unknown

Above: Tourists arriving at Voyageurs National Park, Minnesota, ca. 1925. Photographer unknown. Below: Everglades National Park. Date unknown. Photographer unknown

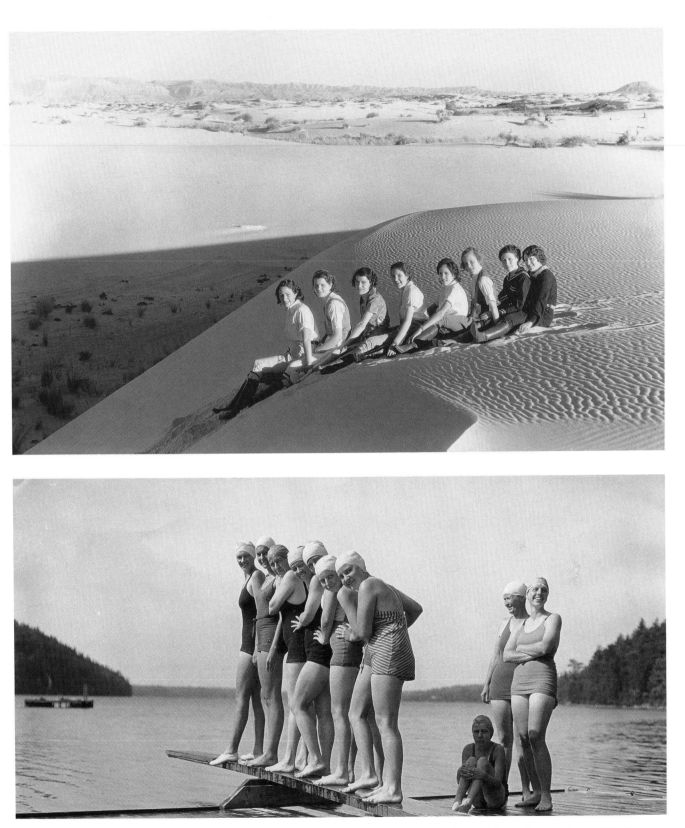

Above: White Sands National Monument, New Mexico, 1934. George A. Grant photo. Below: Acadia National Park, Maine, 1934. Allan Rinehart photo

Above: Chaco Culture National Historical Park, New Mexico, July 24, 1929. George A. Grant Photo
Below: Visitors at "Camp Eielson," Denali National Park, 1944. Allan de Lay photo

Camping at Bear Lake, Rocky Mountain National Park, 1920s. Photographer unknown

Campgrounds and Campfires

Lunchtime in Piegan Pass, Glacier National Park, 1932. George A. Grant photo

Facing page, above: Acadia National Park, 1934. Allan Rinehart photo. Below: Rocky Mountain National Park, early 1900s. Photographer unknown

Above: Campfire at Yosemite, 1936. Ralph Anderson photo.

Left: Mary Roberts Rinehart and party at Glacier, 1920s. Photographer unknown

Tenderfeet attempting to build a fire of petrified wood, Petrified Forest National Park, Arizona, 1929. George A. Grant photo

Fishing in Fall River, Rocky Mountain National Park, 1920s. Photographer unknown

Evolving Views of Wildlife and Nature:
From Fishing Camps to Handkerchief Pools

Facing page, above: Fishing in Olympic National Park, 1938. Brant Report photo
Below, left: Everglades National Park. Date unknown. Photographer unknown Right: Cape Cod National Seashore, 1960s.
Photographer unknown

Deer crossing through campground, Yosemite, 1929. Joseph Dixon photo

Park visitor feeding mule deer buck in Yellowstone, 1926. Photographer unknown

MORNING GLORY POOL

THIS FAR-FAMED POOL HAS EASILY WON ITS NAME FROM THE SYMMETRY AND DEPTH OF ITS CRATER AND THE BLUE COLOR OF THE WATER. THIS BLUE IS THE NORMAL COLOR OF LARGE BODIES OF WATER. THE MORE BRILLIANT HUES TO BE FOUND IN SMALLER QUANTITIES ARE DUE TO A LOW FORM OF PLANT LIFE. WHILE THE FAME OF THIS IS GREAT, IT NEVERTHELESS IS CONSIDERED BY MANY TO BE SURPASSED BY A NUMBER OF OTHER POOLS IN THE PARK, SOME OF WHICH ARE IN THIS GENERAL REGION.

DO NOT THROW OBJECTS IN POOL

Like the feeding of animals, a practice that is discouraged if not prohibited outright in today's parks, tampering with such features as geothermal springs was at one time considered part of the park experience. In the photo at the top of the facing page some visitors of 1934 cook eggs with a ranger over a steam vent in Bumpass Hell, a thermal area in Lassen Volcanic National Park (George A. Grant photo), while a group of 1926 guests at Yellowstone dips handkerchiefs in a sensitive hot spring in the photo below (photographer unknown).

Handkerchief-dipping and other such unfortunate activities were terminated as the parks moved closer to the preservationist management principles of the present day. The photo above shows one outcome of a hot spring clean-up program at Yellowstone in the fall of 1950. Photographer unknown

Without question, the automobile brought people to the national parks in numbers considered unthinkable at the turn of the century, when the preferred way of getting about was in conveyances such as the carriage shown above at Corkscrew Bridge in Yellowstone (photographer unknown).

Automobile Adventurers

Facing page, above: The Holmes Brothers from San Jose drive their Stanley Steamer, the second car to enter Yosemite, in July 1900. J.T. Boysen photo
Below: Western Auto Studebaker Camp Ground Inspection Tour on the "Auto Log" at Sequoia, developed as a tourist attraction after the giant tree fell of natural causes in 1917. Photographer unknown

Above: Colorado Federation of Women's Clubs at Fall River Pass, Rocky Mountain National Park, 1920s. Below: Camping at Aspenglen, Rocky Mountain National Park, 1920s. Photographer unknown. Right: Mount Rainier National Park, 1920s.

Zion Lodge, Zion National Park. George A. Grant photo

Lodges

Right: The Lobby, Many Glacier Hotel, Glacier National Park, 1910s. Photographer unknown

Bryce Canyon National Park, Utah. Date unknown. Photographer unknown

Mount Rainier National Park, 1920s. Photographer unknown

A child gets a better view of the Grand Canyon through the assistance of the National Park Service. Date unknown. Photographer unknown

ACKNOWLEDGMENTS

The publisher gratefully acknowledges the assistance of the following individuals, without whose help this book would not have been possible: Bill Sontag, 75th Anniversary Project Director; Linda Griffin, who assembled the outstanding collection of photographs from which the selections for this book were made; Tom DuRant, Librarian at the NPS Harper's Ferry Center; and John Albright, who cast the eye of the historian over all of the captions. Thanks also to Paul Schullery for contributing a thoughtful essay on the meaning of the National Park Service in its 75th year.

Finally, we would be remiss if we did not acknowledge the great contribution of those early photographers—many of whose names are no longer known to us—who have left us this outstanding chronicle of "one of the best ideas we've ever had."